PROGRAM OVERVIEW

Pre-Kindergarten and Kindergarten

Herbert P. Ginsburg
Carole Greenes
Robert Balfanz

DALE SEYMOUR PUBLICATIONS
Pearson Learning Group

We want to thank the National Science Foundation for all of their encouragement and support. We also want to thank all of the teachers who helped us by field-testing the activities, letting us observe their classrooms, and giving us feedback all along the way.

National Science Foundation

This material is based on work supported by the National Science Foundation under Grant No. ESI-9730683. Any opinions, findings, conclusions, or recommendations expressed here are those of the authors and do not necessarily reflect the views of the National Science Foundation.

The following people have contributed to the development of this product:

Research and Development Team

Boston University, Boston, MA: Kunjan Anjaria, Vanessa Johnson, Michelle Lewis, Susan Looney, Lilla Momtahen, Joan Simpson, Jenny Tsankova

Johns Hopkins University, Baltimore, MD: Dawn Seda

Teachers College, Columbia University, New York, NY: Michelle Galanter, Anna Housley, Joon Lee, Melissa Morganlander, Angelika Yiassemides

Field-Test Teachers and Coordinators

Early Learning Center, Chelsea, MA: Laura Litcofsky, Kristen Rampino, Casey Whiston, Sara Burgin, Diane Loycano, Mary Ann Protasowicki

Boston Public Schools, Boston, MA: Kate Barron, Maria Mendes, Anne Goodrow

Lillie A. Ross Children's Center, Baltimore, MD: Diane Young, Joye Macer, Shatisha Tates, Sherri Simmons

Morning Star Child Development Center, Baltimore, MD: Joan Parker, Carolyn Allen, Wanda Holden

St. Katharine School, Baltimore, MD: Beverly Vaeth, Mary Tobias, Trace Woodson, Tammy Houston

Corpus Christi School, New York, NY: Suzanne Mir

P.S. 207, New York, NY: Elyse Meshnick

University of Wisconsin Children's Center, Milwaukee, WI: Kyoung-Hye Seo, Pam Boulton, Debbie Briggs, Jenni Dykstra, Rae Williams

ISBN 0-7690-2902-7

Printed in the United States of America

8 9 10 11 12 10 09 08 07 06

1-800-321-3106
www.pearsonlearning.com

Contents

Meet the Authors

Herbert P. Ginsburg

Herbert P. Ginsburg is the Jacob H. Schiff Professor of Psychology and Education at Teachers College, Columbia University, where he teaches in the departments of Human Development and Mathematics Education. For many years, he has conducted research on cognitive development, particularly the development of children's mathematical thinking, both nationally and internationally. He has developed several kinds of educational applications, including mathematics textbook series and tests of mathematical thinking. With support from the Spencer Foundation, he recently completed a research project on mathematical competence in young children from different social backgrounds.

Carole Greenes

Carole Greenes is a Professor of Mathematics Education and Associate Dean for Research, Development, and Graduate Programs in the School of Education at Boston University. Principally interested in mathematical problem solving, mathematics learning, and special needs students, Dr. Greenes has written and collaborated on more than 200 books, monographs, and articles in these areas for pre-kindergarten to grade 12 and college mathematics. Dr. Greenes is president of the National Council of Supervisors of Mathematics, a member of the Steering Committee for the NCTM Navigations Series, and a frequent speaker at national and international meetings of mathematicians and mathematics educators.

Robert Balfanz

Robert Balfanz is an Associate Research Scientist at the Center for Social Organization of Schools, Johns Hopkins University. He is one of the developers of an elementary mathematics series and the author of several teacher resource guides for kindergarten to grade 3 mathematics. His current research at the Center for Educating Students Placed at Risk focuses on developing effective instructional programs that combine research-based curricula with multiple tiers of teacher support to accelerate student learning.

A Note About Field-Testing

Big Math for Little Kids® is the culmination of a four-year effort, extending from 1998 to 2002, to create a research-based and developmentally appropriate early childhood mathematics program for all pre-kindergarten and kindergarten children. We began by creating activities that we hoped would engage children in exciting and challenging mathematical explorations and learning in six different areas: numbers, shapes, patterns and logic, measurement, operations on numbers, and spatial relations.

For three years, we informally field-tested these activities in a wide array of preschools and kindergartens in New York, Massachusetts, Maryland, Texas, Wisconsin, and England. The settings included public schools, parochial schools, and early learning centers as well as full-day and half-day programs. Because we wanted Big Math for Little Kids to be effective for children from diverse backgrounds, we worked with minority children from low-income families and children who were just learning English as well as with children from middle-income families. We were fortunate to collaborate with wonderful teachers who allowed us to observe their classrooms, try out activities, videotape what occurred, and interview children. The teachers also gave us their suggestions and evaluations of the activities. During the field-testing, we improved some activities, eliminated others, developed new activities, and arranged the final set into an organized sequence.

During the fourth year of research and development, we began an evaluation of the effectiveness of the program as measured by student achievement and developed methods for helping new teachers learn to implement the program. The result of these four years of work is Big Math for Little Kids, a program that is based in good measure on what we learned from observing children's work with the activities and obtaining teachers' suggestions and evaluations of the program.

We hope you enjoy working with Big Math for Little Kids and that your children have a good deal of fun while learning some exciting ideas!

The Big Math for Little Kids® Authors

The Research Behind the Program

Children's Mathematical Abilities

Big Math for Little Kids® is based on an extensive body of psychological and educational research. For many years, the research of Jean Piaget dominated the fields of developmental psychology and education. Piaget's pioneering work showed that children do not simply receive knowledge from adults, but instead, they construct their own ways of understanding the world (Piaget, 1973).

More recently, psychologists have expanded on Piaget's work in several ways. Their studies show that even infants possess some basic mathematical abilities. In the first year of life, infants can see that a set of two objects is different from a set of three. In early childhood, children can easily determine which of two small collections of objects has "more" than the other. They understand the basics of addition and subtraction, knowing that adding something to a set makes it have more and taking away makes it have fewer.

During the preschool years, young children, regardless of background and culture, develop the same types of mathematical ideas, strategies, and skills. They learn to count, often to very high numbers, and they develop simple methods for calculating sums and differences. The research also shows, however, that young children have difficulty expressing their mathematical thinking. Often they can solve problems in clever ways that they cannot put into words (Ginsburg and Baron, 1992).

Mathematics and Children's Play

Another line of research shows that regardless of background, 4- and 5-year-old children spontaneously engage in several different types of everyday mathematics during free play (Ginsburg, 1999). The activities they most frequently engage in involve pattern and shape. For example, a child builds a block castle with two cylinders representing towers, with a triangular prism on top of each, thereby creating a structure that is symmetrical in three dimensions. The next most frequent types of activities involve magnitude comparison, as when a child insists loudly that his tower is the tallest, and use of number, as when a child points out proudly that she has three dolls or counts to 100.

The Learning Environment

Finally, researchers have revealed the need to examine not only children's current knowledge as measured by various tests, but also children's learning potential. In rich educational environments, particularly when guided by an adult, young children can engage in remarkable investigations of topics like symmetry and pattern (Greenes, 1999).

Research Conclusions

To summarize, modern research has vastly expanded knowledge of young children's mathematical competence. Regardless of background, young children

- possess basic mathematical concepts, strategies, and skills, but have difficulty expressing their thinking in words;
- spontaneously engage in interesting types of mathematical activity during ordinary play;
- can learn a great deal when they are given the opportunity to explore mathematical ideas with adult guidance.

References

Ginsburg, H. P. 1999. Challenging Preschool Education: Meeting the Intellectual Needs of All Children. In *Teaching for Intelligence I: A Collection of Articles.* B. Presseisen, ed. Arlington Heights, IL: Skylight. 287–304.

Ginsburg, H. P., and J. Baron. 1993. Cognition: Young Children's Construction of Mathematics. In *Research Ideas for the Classroom: Early Childhood Education.* R. J. Jensen, ed. New York: Macmillan Publishing Company. 3–21.

Greenes, C. 1999. Ready to Learn: Developing Young Children's Mathematical Powers. In *Mathematics in the Early Years.* J. Copley, ed. Reston, VA: National Council of Teachers of Mathematics. 39–47.

Piaget, J. 1973. *To Understand is to Invent: The Future of Education.* G. and A. Roberts, trans. New York: Grossman.

The Principles Behind the Program

Research studies provide important implications for early childhood mathematics education. They guided the development of the following principles that underlie Big Math for Little Kids.

- *All children are capable of learning mathematics at a young age.* Children do not need to be made ready to learn. They are already engaged in interesting forms of mathematics learning and thinking. They can do informal mathematics, they engage in it freely, and they even enjoy it a great deal. They do mathematics when they play, when they interact with one another, and when they try to understand stories.
- *Play is not enough.* To be sure, children learn through play and should play, but they can only go so far on their own. A large body of psychological research, as well as everyday experience, shows that adult guidance is necessary for children to reach their levels of potential development. The most recent standards of the National Association for the Education of Young Children (Bredekamp and Copple, 1997) concur with this view as does a recent report from the National Research Council (Bowman, Donovan, and Burns, 2001). This does not mean that we should deny children the opportunity to engage in unguided free play. Instead, it means that we should also provide them with adult guidance—in short, we should teach.
- *It is especially important to provide a stimulating preschool and kindergarten environment to low-income children.* Their everyday mathematical activities cry out for attention and nurturance in school. These children need a mathematical head start. They will do well in school if we help them early enough and if we continue to provide good mathematics education.
- *Early childhood mathematics should not involve a push-down curriculum.* For example, excerpts from a first-grade textbook should not be used in a kindergarten classroom. Young children need mathematics education that is developmentally appropriate and enjoyable.
- *Young children are capable of dealing with a comprehensive mathematics curriculum.* They show a spontaneous interest in patterns and shapes, magnitude comparisons, numbers, operations on numbers, classification, and spatial relations. The curriculum for young children should be broad in scope.
- *Young children are capable of dealing with a challenging mathematics curriculum.* They understand the basics of addition and subtraction before entering school, and they often display a spontaneous interest in complex mathematical ideas such as symmetry and large numbers. They are ready to deal with genuinely interesting mathematical ideas.

References

Bowman, B. T., M. S. Donovan, and M. S. Burns, eds. 2001. *Eager to Learn: Educating Our Preschoolers.* Washington, D.C.: National Academy Press.

Bredekamp, S., and C. Copple, eds. 1997. *Developmentally Appropriate Practice in Early Childhood Programs* (revised edition). Washington, D.C.: National Association for the Education of Young Children.

What Does Big Math for Little Kids Offer?

Features

Big Math for Little Kids is a comprehensive and challenging mathematics curriculum with distinct features.

- It draws on young children's everyday mathematical interests and abilities. Big Math for Little Kids is developmentally appropriate and child-centered.
- It provides in-depth, systematic, and sequenced examination of core mathematical topics.
- It naturally integrates mathematics into everyday activities and other academic areas. Big Math for Little Kids integrates mathematics learning into music, art, movement, reading, writing, and classroom routines such as lining up.
- It aims to stimulate playful but purposeful learning. Children have fun doing "Big Math," but their learning is purposeful and results in serious outcomes.
- It employs group instruction, small group teaching, and individual exploration.
- It provides activities that are elaborated over time. Children's attention spans are quite long when they are genuinely interested in a problem.
- It provides practice and repetition.
- It introduces various mathematical symbols and words in careful and meaningful ways.

Benefits

How Children Benefit	How Educators Benefit
Big Math for Little Kids helps children • get ready for elementary school; • learn to love the school learning of mathematics; • learn to think and to become aware of their own thinking; • increase their vocabulary and expressive abilities; • appreciate and understand books; • exercise their intellectual curiosity; • enjoy themselves while learning a great deal of mathematics.	Big Math for Little Kids offers you • clear guidelines for implementing a wide variety of mathematics activities; • activities that are enjoyable, challenging, and organized in a useful sequence; • a variety of optional "more to do" activities; • several practical methods for assessment; • storybooks with interesting mathematical content; • the opportunity to teach your children a great deal of mathematics; • materials for children to take home and use with their families.

The Components of the Program

Big Math for Little Kids provides all the materials you will need to teach mathematics to your pre-kindergarten or kindergarten students. The materials within each level of the program, pre-kindergarten and kindergarten, have been specifically designed to meet the needs of all children in those grades.

The Teacher Resource Binder at each level includes the Program Overview and six Teacher Guides, one for each of the six mathematical units: *What Are Numbers?, The Shape of Things, Patterns Plus, Measure Up!, Working With Numbers,* and *Getting Around.* Teacher Guides include instructional activities, assessment materials, and reproducible masters for creating teaching aids and for providing children with opportunities to practice concepts and skills.

Each grade level also includes six full-color Classroom Storybooks, one for each unit. Take-Home Storybooks, which are black-and-white versions of the Classroom Storybooks, are provided for children to use in school and then take home to share with their families.

Also available is a Big Math for Little Kids manipulative kit for each grade level with materials needed to complete the activities.

Manipulative kits may be purchased from Pearson Learning Group.
Telephone: 1–800–321–3106 Internet: *www.pearsonlearning.com* FAX: 1–800–393–3156

Using the Teacher Guides

Becoming Familiar With the Unit

The first few pages of each Big Math for Little Kids Teacher Guide provide introductory material that describes the unit in detail. These pages can help you become familiar with the mathematical content and instructional goals of the unit as well as the teaching resources that are available within each Teacher Guide.

Using the Activities

Each instructional activity within the Teacher Guides provides all the information you need to help children achieve the goals for the activity. Activity features offer classroom management information, detailed descriptions of mathematical content, and step-by-step instructional guidance.

There are four main sections within each activity. About the Activity includes a preview of the activity and lists the instructional goals. Getting Ready describes what you need to do to prepare for the activity. Let's Go! describes each instructional task within the activity, and More to Do describes how the activity may be extended.

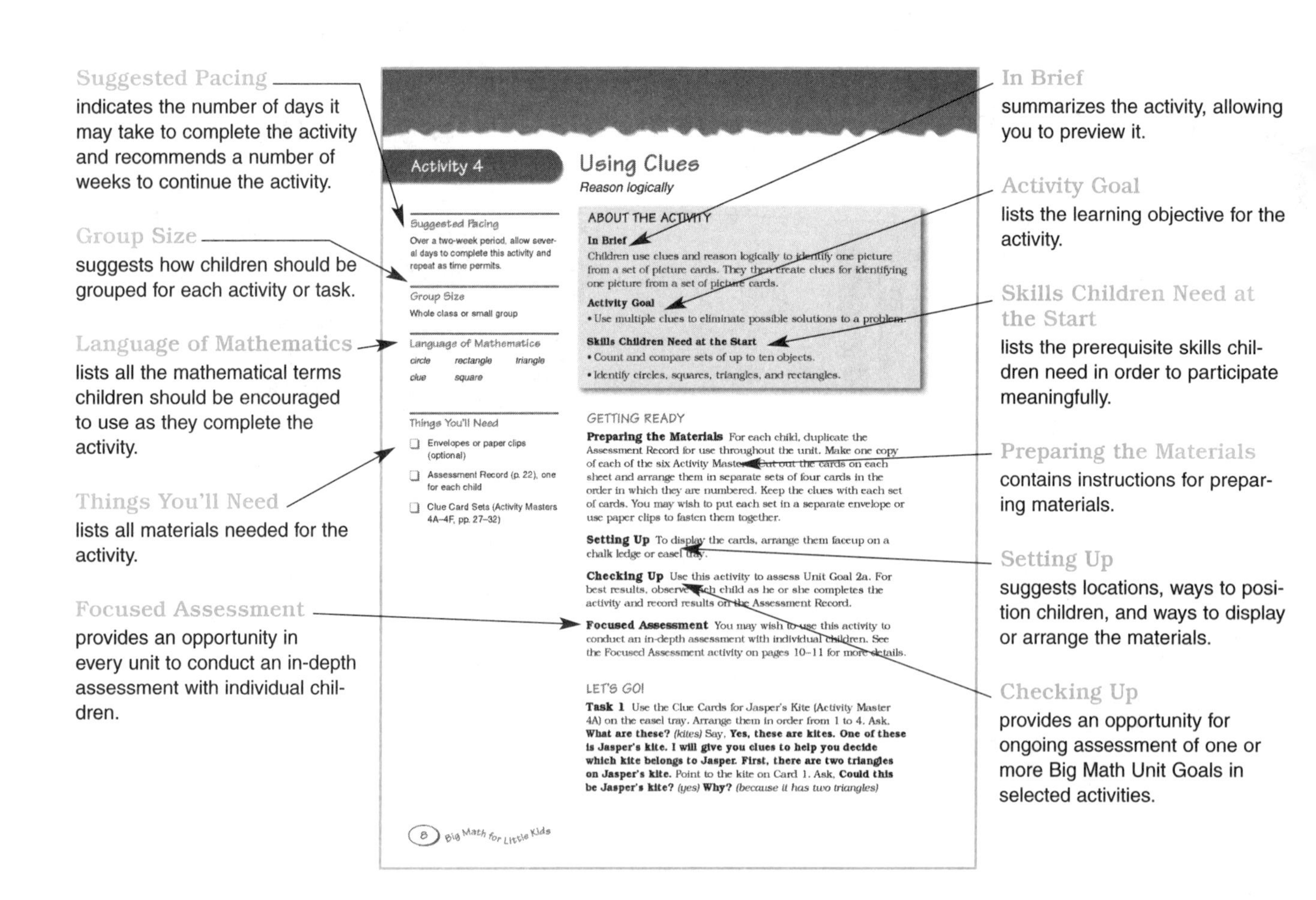

Activity 4

Using Clues

Reason logically

Suggested Pacing

Over a two-week period, allow several days to complete this activity and repeat as time permits.

Group Size

Whole class or small group

Language of Mathematics

circle *rectangle* *triangle* *clue* *square*

Things You'll Need

- Envelopes or paper clips (optional)
- Assessment Record (p. 22), one for each child
- Clue Card Sets (Activity Masters 4A–4F, pp. 27–32)

ABOUT THE ACTIVITY

In Brief
Children use clues and reason logically to identify one picture from a set of picture cards. They then create clues for identifying one picture from a set of picture cards.

Activity Goal
- Use multiple clues to eliminate possible solutions to a problem.

Skills Children Need at the Start
- Count and compare sets of up to ten objects.
- Identify circles, squares, triangles, and rectangles.

GETTING READY

Preparing the Materials For each child, duplicate the Assessment Record for use throughout the unit. Make one copy of each of the six Activity Masters. Cut out the cards on each sheet and arrange them in separate sets of four cards in the order in which they are numbered. Keep the clues with each set of cards. You may wish to put each set in a separate envelope or use paper clips to fasten them together.

Setting Up To display the cards, arrange them faceup on a chalk ledge or easel tray.

Checking Up Use this activity to assess Unit Goal 2a. For best results, observe each child as he or she completes the activity and record results on the Assessment Record.

Focused Assessment You may wish to use this activity to conduct an in-depth assessment with individual children. See the Focused Assessment activity on pages 10–11 for more details.

LET'S GO!

Task 1 Use the Clue Cards for Jasper's Kite (Activity Master 4A) on the easel tray. Arrange them in order from 1 to 4. Ask, **What are these?** *(kites)* Say, **Yes, these are kites. One of these is Jasper's kite. I will give you clues to help you decide which kite belongs to Jasper. First, there are two triangles on Jasper's kite.** Point to the kite on Card 1. Ask, **Could this be Jasper's kite?** *(yes)* **Why?** *(because it has two triangles)*

8 Big Math for Little Kids

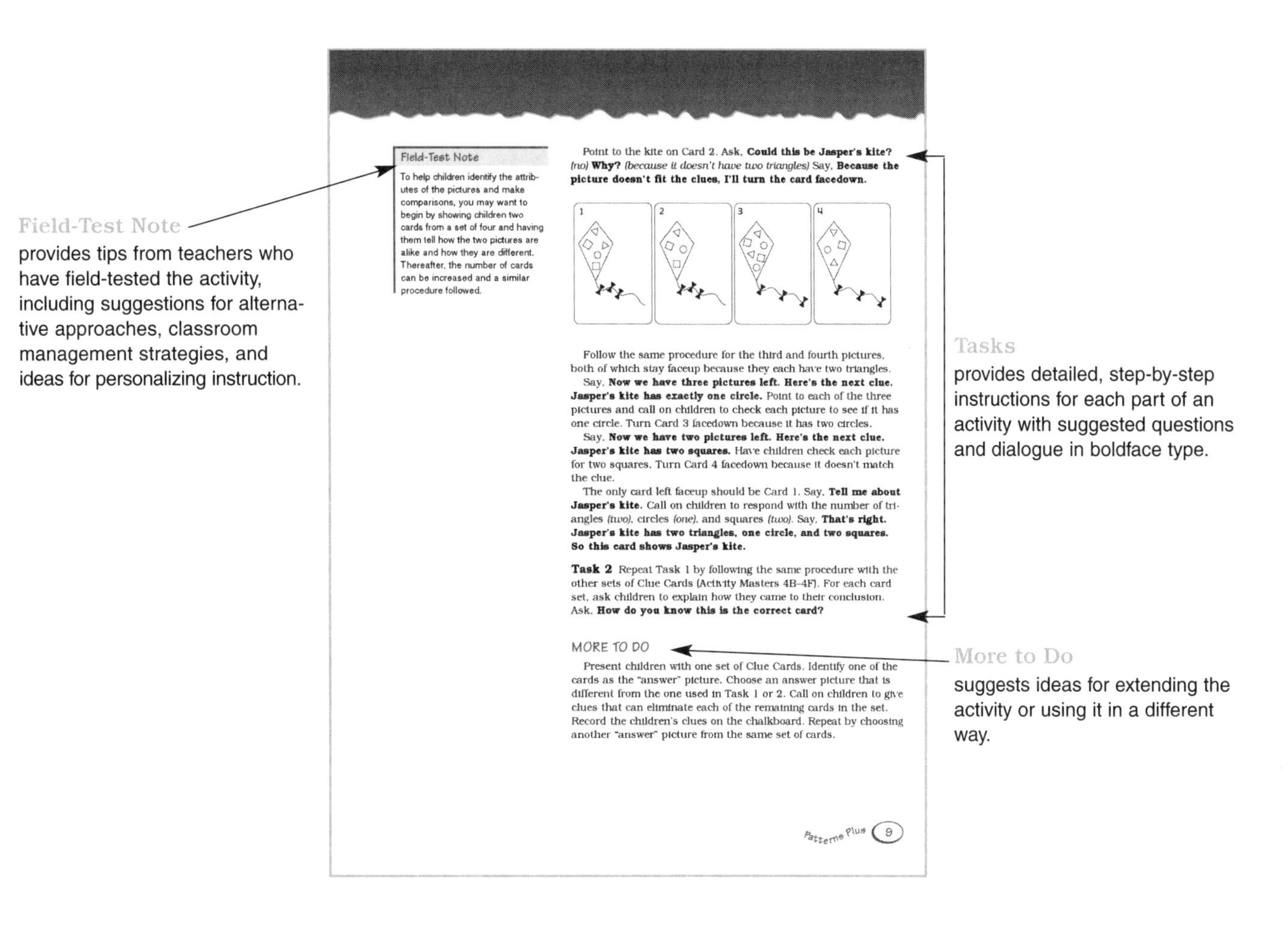

Field-Test Note

To help children identify the attributes of the pictures and make comparisons, you may want to begin by showing children two cards from a set of four and having them tell how the two pictures are alike and how they are different. Thereafter, the number of cards can be increased and a similar procedure followed.

Point to the kite on Card 2. Ask, **Could this be Jasper's kite?** *(no)* **Why?** *(because it doesn't have two triangles)* Say, **Because the picture doesn't fit the clues, I'll turn the card facedown.**

Follow the same procedure for the third and fourth pictures, both of which stay faceup because they each have two triangles.

Say, **Now we have three pictures left. Here's the next clue. Jasper's kite has exactly one circle.** Point to each of the three pictures and call on children to check each picture to see if it has one circle. Turn Card 3 facedown because it has two circles.

Say, **Now we have two pictures left. Here's the next clue. Jasper's kite has two squares.** Have children check each picture for two squares. Turn Card 4 facedown because it doesn't match the clue.

The only card left faceup should be Card 1. Say, **Tell me about Jasper's kite.** Call on children to respond with the number of triangles *(two)*, circles *(one)*, and squares *(two)*. Say, **That's right. Jasper's kite has two triangles, one circle, and two squares. So this card shows Jasper's kite.**

Task 2 Repeat Task 1 by following the same procedure with the other sets of Clue Cards (Activity Masters 4B–4F). For each card set, ask children to explain how they came to their conclusion. Ask, **How do you know this is the correct card?**

MORE TO DO

Present children with one set of Clue Cards. Identify one of the cards as the "answer" picture. Choose an answer picture that is different from the one used in Task 1 or 2. Call on children to give clues that can eliminate each of the remaining cards in the set. Record the children's clues on the chalkboard. Repeat by choosing another "answer" picture from the same set of cards.

Patterns Plus 9

Using the Reproducible Masters

Several kinds of reproducible masters are provided at the back of each unit.

- A Family Letter, available in English and in Spanish, shows family members what children will be learning in that unit of the Big Math for Little Kids program.
- The Take-Home Game, also available in English and in Spanish, allows children to practice concepts and skills at home.
- The Assessment Record enables you to record the results of assessment of unit concepts and skills.
- Activity Masters, including teaching aids and practice pages, provide opportunities for children to practice new concepts and skills. For ease of use, these pages are numbered according to the activity in which they are used rather than consecutively.

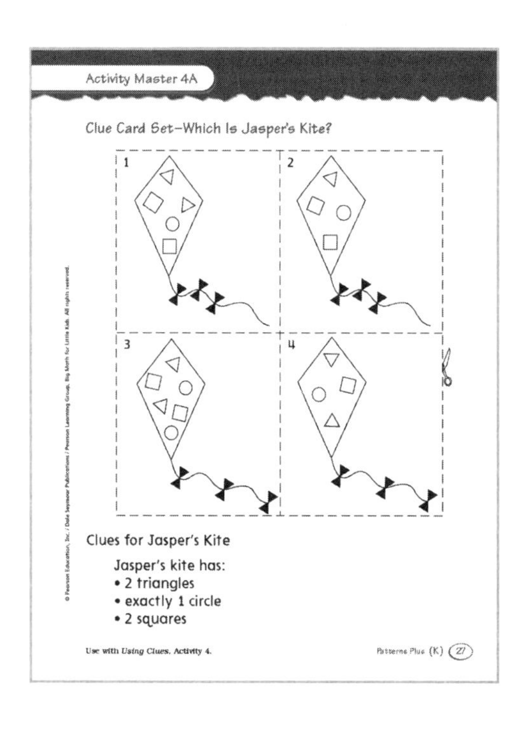

Activity Master 4A

Clue Card Set–Which Is Jasper's Kite?

1 2 3 4

Clues for Jasper's Kite

Jasper's kite has:
- 2 triangles
- exactly 1 circle
- 2 squares

Use with *Using Clues,* Activity 4. Patterns Plus (K) 27

Using the Storybooks

The Classroom Storybooks for Big Math for Little Kids facilitate children's language development while introducing them to new mathematical ideas or providing them with opportunities to practice and demonstrate what they know. Field-testing has shown that the books are very enjoyable, too—children love to hear them read again and again.

Content of the Stories

Each of the Big Math units includes a full-color Classroom Storybook that highlights one or more key ideas in the unit. The table below lists the story for each unit and the key mathematical concept(s) behind the story.

Unit	Pre-Kindergarten	Kindergarten
Unit 1: *What Are Numbers?*	*Henrietta Sees Numbers* (recognizing the number of objects in a set without counting)	*So Many Fives!* (representing numbers in different ways)
Unit 2: *The Shape of Things*	*The Trees of Mrs. McGee* (identifying basic shapes)	*Favorite Shapes* (attributes of basic shapes)
Unit 3: *Patterns Plus*	*The Table of Phinneas Fable* (shape patterns)	*Dobee Doubler* (patterns with doubled numbers)
Unit 4: *Measure Up!*	*Jenny Saves the Day* (pennies and nickels)	*Tick-Tock!* (relating time and daily activities)
Unit 5: *Working With Numbers*	*Acorn Hunt* (comparing, adding, and subtracting)	*Leftover Muffins* (making equal shares)
Unit 6: *Getting Around*	*Rafael's Messy Room* (positions and locations)	*Two-Two the Tooth Fairy* (maps and directions)

Interacting With the Stories

The Classroom Storybooks are introduced as part of an activity in every unit. The stories are intended to be used in an interactive way, such as encouraging children to chime in on rhyming or repetitive sections. Though they are not expected to read the storybooks, some children, especially at the kindergarten level, may attempt to read common words and mathematical symbols on their own.

The Take-Home Storybooks

Each of the Big Math for Little Kids Classroom Storybooks has a companion Take-Home Storybook. After hearing and participating in the classroom story several times, children are given their own Take-Home Storybooks. Each of these provides the same story as the classroom book, but in a black-and-white version that children can color and that often omits a few illustrations so that children can complete them.

Children use the Take-Home Storybooks for classroom follow-up activities that enable them to consolidate their learning. Children are encouraged to take the books home, explain what they have learned, and read the story again with family members. Included in each Take-Home Storybook is a letter to the family with suggestions on how to use the book at home.

The Mathematical Content

The mathematical content of the pre-kindergarten and kindergarten levels of Big Math for Little Kids is organized around the same six mathematical strands or units. The kindergarten units build on the concepts and skills that are introduced at the pre-kindergarten level.

Unit 1: *What Are Numbers?*

Three major topics are highlighted in this unit at each level: the counting sequence, the use of numbers to tell how many objects are in a group, and the use of ordinal numbers to identify the position of an object in a line or of an event in a sequence of events. With the aid of body movements, children learn the counting sequence, counting by ones to 10 and then to 20. Once they have mastered the "yucky teens" (11 to 19), they learn rules for counting to 50. In kindergarten they extend their skills by counting to greater numbers and then by tens, fives, and twos as well. At both grade levels they learn to count on from a number other than one.

Children apply counting skills to identify the number of objects in a group or the cardinality of the group. They learn that the size, shape, color, function, and physical arrangement of objects in a group do not affect the count, and that the last item counted tells the total number in the group. Recording numerals and matching numerals to groups of objects are also emphasized. These skills are also reinforced in activities in other units. For example, in *The Shape of Things*, both levels, children count to tell the number of straight sides of two-dimensional shapes. In *Measure Up!*, level Pre-K, children use pennies and nickels to show small amounts such as six cents. At level K, children count pennies, nickels, and dimes to find the total number of cents. In both levels of *Patterns Plus*, children count the elements in the part of the pattern that repeats.

The third topic is ordinal numbers. Children learn to identify the first, second, third, and last objects in a line in level Pre-K, and the first through tenth objects in level K. Through explorations, they learn that what is first and last depends on the point of view. The ability to identify a sequence of events over time, that is, to tell what happens first, second, third, and last, is important when describing sequences of rhythmic actions in *Patterns Plus* and in actions of combining (adding, multiplying) and separating (subtracting, dividing) in *Working With Numbers*.

Unit 2: *The Shape of Things*

Activities in this unit engage children in the identification of two- and three-dimensional shapes, in the examination of attributes of these shapes, and in exploration of the symmetry of shapes. Children learn to identify circles, triangles, squares, nonsquare rectangles, pentagons, and hexagons of various sizes and in varying positions. They learn that squares are special types of rectangles. They count and compare the numbers of corners and straight sides of the shapes. They search for and identify examples of spheres, cubes, rectangular prisms (that are not cubes), and cylinders in the classroom. In level K, their search is extended to include pyramids, cones, and triangular prisms, and students learn to identify the shapes of the faces of these three-dimensional objects. Two-dimensional shapes are constructed and taken apart, and towers are constructed from two-dimensional pictures of the towers. Finally, lines of symmetry of circles, triangles, squares, and rectangles are identified.

Unit 3: *Patterns Plus*

The focus of this unit is on repeating patterns in level Pre-K, repeating and growing patterns in level K, and on logical reasoning in both levels. Children explore repeating patterns such as ABAB and growing patterns such as 2, 4, 6, 8 that involve shape, size, number, letter, color, rhythm, or pitch. Children copy, complete, extend, and describe patterns, and use their descriptions to predict what comes next. They learn to represent patterns in different ways, for example, with drawings and color blocks.

Logical reasoning is developed as children use clues to eliminate candidates for the solution to a problem. For example, in the pre-kindergarten activity, Who Is Mr. Glump?, the goal is to figure out which picture shows the real Mr. Glump. As a clue is given, children check each picture to determine if it fits the clue. If it does not, it is eliminated from consideration. The activities in this unit require the application of counting skills and shape identification skills.

Unit 4: *Measure Up!*

Children explore ideas dealing with length, weight, capacity, temperature, time, and money in this unit. Greatest attention is placed on comparing lengths and heights, and on measuring and ordering objects by length and height. Children learn that a common endpoint must be used to make length and height comparisons. After a great deal of comparison experience, they first learn to use nonstandard units (blocks) and then standard units (inches) in level K to find measures of length.

Children explore concepts of weight by comparing weights of objects by hand and by using pan balances. They learn that a level pan balance shows same or equal weights and use nonstandard units to obtain weight measurements for a variety of objects. Capacity comparisons are carried out at both grade levels by pouring the contents of one container into another. In level K, children learn to use nonstandard units (scoops) and then standard units (cups) to measure the capacity of containers.

For temperature, pre-kindergarten children associate clothing of different kinds with hot and cold temperatures. Kindergarten children compare the warmth of buckets of water. Later, they learn to associate greater numbers on a thermometer with warmer temperatures and lesser numbers with colder temperatures.

Time explorations at level Pre-K consist of identifying the segments of a day (morning, afternoon, night) and interpreting calendars. At level K, children's understanding is extended as they learn to read and interpret analog and digital clocks, make hourly schedules, and identify dates on a calendar.

Money, that is, coins and their values, is also explored in this unit. Children first learn to identify pennies and nickels from both heads and tails views. At the kindergarten level they also explore dimes and the relationships between values of pairs of coins, for example, 5 pennies = 1 nickel; 2 nickels = 1 dime.

Unit 5: Working With Numbers

In this unit, children are introduced to combining and separating types of problems. Addition, subtraction, and later, multiplication and division situations are explored and modeled using stories, games, and manipulatives. Children combine groups of objects to determine a sum or total in level Pre-K, then also decompose numbers to find pairs of numbers that produce a given sum in level K. They explore subtraction by comparing two groups to tell which has more and by "taking away" a subset of a group and identifying the number left. Children learn to tell addition and subtraction stories, and in level K, they begin to write addition and subtraction number sentences. Multiplication is introduced in level K as repeated addition of equal groups. Division is modeled in both grade levels by the equal sharing of a group of objects.

Unit 6: Getting Around

Activities in this unit at each grade level focus on the development of spatial concepts and on the related skill of map-making. Children learn to identify and describe relative positions of objects using positional vocabulary such as *on top of, next to, between, in front of, behind, to the left,* and *to the right.* In level Pre-K, children learn to read a map of the classroom and use the map to locate objects. At level K, children construct maps to show the location and relative distances between various objects in their classroom. They learn to "read" a map and to locate objects in their classroom. They also learn to give oral directions for locating particular objects.

The Scope and Sequence that follows presents a detailed list and comparison of skills for each of the pre-kindergarten and kindergarten units. The chart includes teacher guide page references for each skill.

Scope and Sequence

UNIT 1: *What Are Numbers?*

	Pre-Kindergarten Teacher Guide	Kindergarten Teacher Guide
Counting		
by ones up to 50	1–21, 29–30	1–2
by ones to 100		8–11
by tens to 100	20–21	8–11, 20–21
by fives to 100		8–11, 20–21
by ones from a number other than 1	13–14	1–2, 10–11
Counting to tell how many		
up to 10 objects	2–7, 9–12, 15–19 29–30	
up to 15 objects		3–7, 12–14
match numbers to sets of objects	9–12, 29–30	6–7, 12–16
Comparing sets		
use one-to-one correspondence	6–7	6–7
identify same, more, fewer	6–7	3–7, 17–19, 26–27
more than, less than		17–19
use a graph to compare numbers		17–18
Reading, writing, representing numbers		
represent numbers in different ways	9–10, 15–19, 29–30	5, 17–18, 22–27
write numerals 0 to 10		22–27
read word names for numbers 0 to 12		12–16, 19, 22–25
Ordinal numbers and position		
before, after, between, front, back, next, last	9–10, 13–17, 20–23, 26–28	12–14, 20–21 28–34
identify first to sixth	22–23, 26–27	
identify first to tenth		28–31
identify position of events in a sequence	24–25, 28	32–34

UNIT 2: *The Shape of Things*

	Pre-Kindergarten Teacher Guide	Kindergarten Teacher Guide
Two-dimensional shapes		
recognize circles, squares, triangles, rectangles, hexagons, pentagons	1–8, 11–12	1–10, 13–14
use shape vocabulary	1–8	1–10, 13–14, 17–24
count sides and corners	3–10	1–2, 7–12
recognize common attributes		13–14
recognize squares as rectangles	6	1–2, 5–6
match shapes and names		7–10, 13–14
Symmetry		
match halves at line of symmetry	13–14	
identify lines of symmetry of polygons		17–18
Three-dimensional shapes		
recognize cubes, rectangular prisms, cylinders, spheres	15–16	19–20, 23–24
recognize square pyramids, triangular prisms		21–22
use shape vocabulary	15–16	19–24
identify faces of three-dimensional shapes		21–22

UNIT 3: *Patterns Plus*

	Pre-Kindergarten Teacher Guide	Kindergarten Teacher Guide
Patterns		
identify, create, copy, and extend sound patterns	9–10	5–7
identify, create, and extend color patterns	1–2	13
identify, create, and extend shape patterns	5–8	12
identify patterns with color and shape		12–13
identify and extend letter patterns		3–4
identify, create, and extend number patterns	3–4	16–18
identify, create, and extend growing and decreasing patterns	10	16–18
identify patterns with doubles		1–2
identify position of objects within a pattern	1–2, 5–8	3–4
Logic		
Reason logically	11–12	8–11

UNIT 4: *Measure Up!*

	Pre-Kindergarten Teacher Guide	Kindergarten Teacher Guide
Length		
compare height and length of two or more objects	1-6	1-8
order objects by length or height		1-8
use comparative vocabulary: *same length/height; tall, taller, tallest; short, shorter, shortest; long, longer, longest; far, farther, farthest*	1-6	1-8
recognize the relationship between height and length		1-4
use nonstandard units to measure and compare length		5-8
use inches to measure and compare length		9-10
Weight		
use a pan balance	9-10	11-16
explore methods for achieving balance		11-12, 15-16
compare weight of two or more objects	7-10	11-18
use comparative vocabulary: *same weight; heavy, heavier, heaviest; light, lighter, lightest*	7-10	11-18
order objects by weight		11-16
compare weight and size		17-18
use nonstandard units to measure and compare weight		15-16
Capacity		
identify more and less	11-12	19-20
order containers by capacity		19-20
use comparative vocabulary	11-12	19-22
use nonstandard units to measure and compare capacities		19-20
explore relationships among quarts, cups, and half-cups		21-22
recognize the relationship between size and capacity		21-22

UNIT 4: *Measure Up! continued*

	Pre-Kindergarten Teacher Guide	Kindergarten Teacher Guide
Temperature		
compare temperatures		23–24
use comparative vocabulary: *hot, warm, cool, cold*	13–14	23–24
associate outdoor events with hot or cold temperatures	13–14	23–24
use a Fahrenheit thermometer		23–24
Time		
morning, afternoon, night	15–16	
associate activities with time of day	15–16	25–28
today, tomorrow, yesterday	17–18	
tell time to the hour on analog and digital clocks		25–28
explore meaning of a minute		29–30
use a calendar	17–18	31–33
order events	15–16	34–35
use temporal vocabulary: *first, second, . . . last; before, after, between*	15–16	31–35
Money		
identify and name pennies and nickels	19–21	36–37
identify and name dimes		36–37
identify the values of pennies and nickels	19–21	38–39
identify the values of dimes		38–39
trade pennies for nickels and dimes		38–39

UNIT 5: *Working With Numbers*

	Pre-Kindergarten Teacher Guide	Kindergarten Teacher Guide
Comparing numbers		
compare sets to identify more and fewer	1–2, 11–20	1–5
identify how many more or fewer	1–2, 11–20	1–5
use a bar graph to compare numbers	18–20	

UNIT 5: *Working With Numbers, continued*

	Pre-Kindergarten Teacher Guide	Kindergarten Teacher Guide
Operating with numbers		
add and subtract 1 from a set	1–20	3–8, 17–18
add to 12 with concrete objects	1–5, 11–12	6–8
use repeated addition		19–21
subtract with concrete objects	1–2, 6–17	3–5, 12–18
partition numbers into addends		9–11, 24–25
separate a set into two equal groups	21–22	22–23
share objects equally among more than two groups		22–23
find number families through 9		9–11
Representing numbers and operations		
use counters to represent objects	3–5	1–21
identify and use the + and – symbols		6–14, 17–18
write addition and subtraction sentences		6–8, 12–14, 17–18
identify ones, tens, and hundreds		26–27

UNIT 6: *Getting Around*

	Pre-Kindergarten Teacher Guide	Kindergarten Teacher Guide
Positions and locations		
right and left	1–2, 5–8, 13–16	1–2, 5–6, 11–19
forward and backward	5–8	5–6, 14–15, 18–19
inside, next, behind, in front	3–4, 7–8, 13–14	3–4, 7–13
bottom, middle, top, over, under	3–4, 7–16	3–4, 7–10, 16–17
Directions		
follow and identify directions	5–8, 13–14	3–6, 14–15
Maps		
use a map to identify location	17–18	11–13
make a map		11–13

Meeting the Standards

The authors of Big Math for Little Kids have been at the center of efforts to develop research-based guidelines on the type and level of mathematical activities that are beneficial to young children. They have consulted with the National Association for the Education of Young Children (NAEYC) in the development of the joint position statement with the National Council of Teachers of Mathematics (NCTM) on early childhood mathematics. The Big Math for Little Kids authors helped to organize and participated in the National Science Foundation's Conference on Early Math Standards, held in May 2000, which brought together early childhood leaders from 40 state Departments of Education to discuss early childhood state math standards.

Drawing on these experiences, the authors have been careful to align Big Math for Little Kids with both the NCTM standards and the joint position statement of NCTM and NAEYC on early childhood mathematics. A table showing the alignment between Big Math for Little Kids and the NCTM standards is provided below. Furthermore, Big Math for Little Kids has been aligned with state and district standards for pre-kindergarten and kindergarten mathematics. The Scope and Sequence on pages 14–18 has been benchmarked against existing state standards. Although the specificity and scope of many state and district pre-kindergarten and kindergarten mathematics standards are still evolving, the authors are confident that Big Math for Little Kids will meet and, in most cases, exceed those standards.

NCTM Standards

1. Number and Operations
2. Algebra
3. Geometry
4. Measurement
5. Data Analysis and Probability
6. Problem Solving
7. Reasoning and Proof
8. Communication
9. Connections
10. Representation

Big Math for Little Kids

Unit 1: *What Are Numbers?*	Standards 1, 6–10
Unit 2: *The Shape of Things*	Standards 3, 6–10
Unit 3: *Patterns Plus*	Standards 2, 5–10
Unit 4: *Measure Up!*	Standards 4, 6–10
Unit 5: *Working With Numbers*	Standards 1, 5–10
Unit 6: *Getting Around*	Standards 3, 6–10

Implementing the Program

Most of the pre-kindergarten and kindergarten teachers who field-tested Big Math for Little Kids had little experience in teaching mathematics. Indeed, some of the teachers were somewhat leery of mathematics and lacked confidence in their abilities to teach it well. However, within a short time, they learned how to use the program successfully and enjoyed it a great deal. The next three pages provide suggestions and strategies for implementing the program based on their experiences.

Involving the Family

After becoming familiar with Big Math for Little Kids, many of the field-test teachers held special meetings to introduce the program to the children's families. Recognizing the importance the family plays in successful school learning, these teachers felt that parent support would be extremely beneficial. Teachers explained that the children would be engaging in challenging mathematics activities and would be bringing home storybooks to share with them. The teachers also shared some of the family letters describing the activities that family members might do with the children. An important message to convey to families is not to drill the children, not push them too much, nor expect them to learn everything. Instead, convince parents that their job is to enjoy learning "big math" with their children.

Deciding When and How to Begin

How did the teachers do it? They waited a few weeks after school began to introduce children to Big Math for Little Kids. When children were functioning well in the classroom and understood routines such as "circle time," the teachers introduced the program beginning with Unit 1, *What are Numbers?*, specifically the first activity involving counting (Count, Clap, and Stomp for pre-kindergarten, and Fancy Number Chants for kindergarten). Little children tend to think of math as learning numbers or learning to count, and they believe that counting "high" is a grown-up thing to do. They really enjoy counting activities. Of course, there is much more to math than counting, as children in the program soon learn. It is recommended that regardless of level, you begin with Unit 1 and then introduce the units in the numbered sequence designated. After you have had some experience with the program, you may choose to vary the sequence.

Establishing Big Math Routines

As the field-test teachers went through the first several activities, they learned how to make effective use of different classroom organizations. Most of the teachers introduced Big Math for Little Kids activities during circle time, which typically was the first activity of the day. Teachers often began circle time by having children greet each other, note who was absent, talk about the day of the month, and mark it on the calendar. They then moved into a Big Math for Little Kids activity suitable for the whole class.

After that, the children often went to work in small groups. The teacher led at least one of these groups. Sometimes the teacher, particularly at the kindergarten level, managed to supervise more than one group at the same time. Sometimes assistants also worked with small groups on another Big Math activity or a non-math activity. The small group work enabled teachers to learn about individual children's progress and to provide appropriate assistance. Occasionally, small group activities led teachers to work with individual children who were having difficulty or who required more challenging experiences. For example, one teacher learned that a pre-kindergarten child was particularly fascinated with written numbers. For this child, the teacher wrote numbers on squares of construction paper, and the child spent considerable time during free play trying to arrange the numbers in order.

Usually teachers identified time devoted to Big Math for Little Kids as "special time." One teacher even prepared distinctive tags for children to wear during Big Math activities. Children felt that Big Math for Little Kids was special and liked to have it identified as such. They wanted to do math just like the "big kids."

After circle time and small group work familiarized children with the activity, teachers sometimes placed the materials in a special "center," or area, where children might use them during free play. At this time, many children chose to play games like "Monster Mountain," to "read" the storybooks, or to create patterns with colored blocks.

Teachers tended to read the Big Math storybooks during circle time and on other special occasions. They found that children enjoyed hearing the books read to them many times. This repetition also ensured that children understood the book before taking home individual copies to "read" and explain to family members.

Making Curriculum Choices

One big issue that many of the teachers faced as they learned to implement Big Math for Little Kids was how much to do. How were they to do all of the activities in the time available? Their experience led them to conclude that it is possible to do the entire Big Math for Little Kids curriculum if they were willing to spend 30 to 40 minutes a day on the activities. Though the complete program is appropriate for both full-day and half-day classrooms, activities can be limited and chosen to meet teacher and student needs. The planning charts in each Teacher Guide can be very helpful for this purpose.

Teachers used more and more of the program each year they worked with Big Math for Little Kids. After a period of time, one teacher said that math was now her favorite subject (and her students') and that she could do, and often did, Big Math for Little Kids several times a day.

Scheduling Instructional Time

The planning chart and the suggested pacing feature in each activity give approximate guidelines for pacing the activities. For example, the chart may indicate that the activity should be implemented over a week's time and the pacing feature may indicate that the tasks within an activity generally take one or more days. Pacing should be devised to meet individual needs. It is suggested that you review the tasks for an activity, consider the number and size of the instructional groups you will form, and estimate how long each task should take. These steps will help you complete a realistic schedule of activities.

Learning Expectations

Related to pacing is the issue of how much you should expect children to master during the course of the program. You should not expect young children to learn the same things at the same time nor to learn everything immediately. Children learn at different rates. The field-test teachers noticed that some children did not seem to be learning anything for a while but then seemed suddenly to "get it." Some children did not learn all of the ideas. We want children to learn some basic concepts and skills, but it is rare for children to learn everything that is introduced in Big Math for Little Kids. So give children many chances to learn and don't worry if they don't show immediate mastery.

Adapting the Program to Your Classroom

Some of the field-test teachers were faced with interesting challenges and coped with them in productive ways.

- *Kindergarten children who do not seem ready.* Several of the teachers felt that their kindergarten children were not ready for the kindergarten level of Big Math for Little Kids. Their solution was to have both levels of the program available. They began with several of the corresponding pre-kindergarten activities before introducing the kindergarten activities. For example, several of these teachers began with the pre-kindergarten counting activity Count, Clap, and Stomp before introducing the kindergarten counting activity Fancy Number Chants. Similarly, they introduced the pre-kindergarten cardinality activity Bag It before bumping the level up to the kindergarten version of the activity. In general, these teachers found that providing their children with extra foundation work was necessary. Also, these teachers remarked that although many of the children did not seem to be "getting" the material at the outset, they did eventually seem to learn a great deal. In this situation, patience and optimism are essential. The children are capable and will eventually perform well at the kindergarten level.
- *Pre-kindergarten children who seem to need extra work.* Several of the teachers felt that their pre-kindergarten children were capable of doing a higher level of work than what is expected in the pre-kindergarten level of Big Math for Little Kids. Their solution was also to have both levels of the program available. They decided to introduce various kindergarten level activities at appropriate points. For example, after their pre-kindergarten children counted by ones to 50 in Numbers with Pizzazz, teachers introduced the kindergarten activity Fancy Number Chants. Basically, these teachers went beyond the pre-kindergarten More to Do suggestions to introduce what they felt was appropriate kindergarten content.
- *What to do with 3-year-olds.* Several teachers had 3-year-olds in their classrooms. After considerable thought and experimentation, teachers decided to introduce these children to the pre-kindergarten program, but did not expect them to learn it at the same level as the 4-year-olds. This decision removed the pressure from both teachers and children. With final evaluation of children's progress, the teachers were surprised to learn that many 3-year-olds had learned a great deal and those who did not had received a good foundation for the next year's work.

Assessing Children's Mathematical Learning

What Is Assessment?

Assessment is developing an understanding of the children in your class. Assessment is discovering what children are doing, what they know and understand, what they are learning and having trouble learning, and how they solve problems. Assessment is discovering what children are interested in, what they are feeling, and what motivates them. Assessment is discovering how children change over time and gradually—and sometimes mysteriously—learn what you are teaching.

As teachers, we engage in informal assessment all the time in our everyday interactions with children. We observe that Lisa looks confused when she tries to play a game. We see that Keith does not point to each marble he is counting and therefore gets the wrong answer. We ask Alexandra how she got the answer to a problem and she has difficulty describing her steps. All of these informal perceptions and judgments are forms of assessment. We frequently observe, listen, and talk with children to learn what they know and don't know.

Many teachers of young children are leery of assessment. They think of assessment as unnecessary, pressured testing. However, that is not the kind of assessment offered in Big Math for Little Kids. In this program, assessment is not testing. It is not an attempt to compare a child with others in the classroom or with a national norming group. It is not an attempt to place children in categories such as slow learner, or to label them as "not ready for school." Instead, it is simply getting to know your children as well as you can.

Difficulties of Assessment

Assessing children is not easy. Sometimes they are tired, find it hard to express their ideas in words, seem to be in another world that you can't enter, refuse to talk with you, or are shy. They may not understand what you are saying or asking them to do. Their responses may be inconsistent. Their development may be uneven, so that one day they may seem to know something, but on the next they do not appear to understand the same concept. They may show spurts of concentrated attention, but then may seem indifferent for a period of time. Perhaps the most difficult aspect of assessment is that children see the world differently from the way adults do. It is very hard for the teacher to imagine that a child might believe that the sun is following her around all day or that five toys in a line have a different number from the same five toys arranged in a circle.

Beyond all of these typical difficulties, you may encounter special assessment challenges. Children from some cultures may feel that it is improper to talk with an adult and believe that to show respect they need to remain silent. Children with disabilities may be difficult to assess because their hearing is limited or they experience distinctive language difficulties.

Benefits of Assessment

Despite all of these difficulties, it is very important for you to assess your children's learning. There are several important reasons for assessment.

- Assessment is necessary for effective teaching. Good teaching elaborates on, expands, and systematizes children's informal knowledge and everyday interests. It is responsive to children's efforts at learning, to their understandings and confusions. Good teaching, in short, depends on sensitive assessment of children's learning.
- Assessment can help you identify special learning difficulties that children sometimes face. One child may have trouble dealing with verbal material and another with tasks requiring fine motor coordination. You need to be alert for reasons why children sometimes have trouble learning.
- Assessment can provide you with useful information to communicate with parents or other teachers who may then work with and help the child.

Principles of Assessment

Some basic principles inform the Big Math for Little Kids approach to assessment.

- No one type of assessment can provide all the information you need about a child. You need to use several methods to get to know what a child is thinking and learning.
- It is important to listen and observe how children behave in their everyday environment and during activities that you introduce. You can learn a great deal from observing children's free play and how they engage in learning activities.
- Occasionally listening and observing—what is sometimes called performance assessment—are not sufficient. Children's speech and behavior do not always reveal what they really know. It is often important to question children about their work.
- It is acceptable if children do not achieve mastery in all areas. Although it is important to expose children to a wide range of mathematical ideas and give them an opportunity to learn, children are not expected to learn everything. Children are expected, however, to learn *some* big mathematical ideas.
- Do not expect children in your class to learn the same things at the same time. There is enormous variability within and among children in the early years. Some children do not seem to "get it" at all on one day and then several days later seem to have learned. Some children in the group will be interested and involved, and others will not.
- As you assess, do no harm. Do not pressure the children. Don't place them in threatening testlike conditions. You need to treat them gently and assess them informally.

Three Kinds of Assessment

Big Math for Little Kids provides three types of assessment, each serving a particular purpose.

- *Checking Up* involves observation of children's learning during selected activities. For example, you can observe group or individual work during an activity on patterns in order to determine whether a child has a basic understanding of the key concept of repeating patterns. Checking Up helps you observe whether children have attained important learning objectives.
- *Focused Assessment* provides you with an extended opportunity to examine an individual child's understanding of a key learning objective. A Focused Assessment activity appears once in every unit. You may wish to use Focused Assessment when you are unsure of a child's abilities or are concerned about a child's progress and want to determine how to help. Focused Assessment involves two components. One is observation of a child's performance during an activity that involves important concepts and skills. A second component is an interview that you can conduct to clarify the nature of the child's understanding.
- *Continuing Assessment* provides you with an opportunity to reexamine children's knowledge of key concepts involving number, shape, and measurement. Specific activities in Units 1, 2, and 4 have been designated to be repeated at regular intervals throughout the school year. Observation of students' mathematical behavior during the activities will allow you to determine whether children retain basic skills such as counting or recognizing numerals.

These three types of assessment can contribute in important ways to supporting your teaching.

Developing the Whole Child

Big Math for Little Kids was designed to develop a wide range of skills, behaviors, and motivations that are essential to both the mathematical and overall development of young children.

Social Behavior

Many of the mathematical activities in Big Math for Little Kids are inherently social. They involve children working cooperatively in both small and large groups. Throughout the program, children learn how to share their thoughts and findings, take turns, listen, and follow established procedures. The program helps to socialize children for schooling.

Motivation

At the heart of Big Math for Little Kids is the idea that children should encounter situations that provoke learning. As they grapple with challenging problems, children learn the value of perseverance and the benefit of effort. As they experience success in learning mathematics, children's self-confidence grows.

Another key principle of Big Math for Little Kids is that mistakes should be treated as avenues for learning. This teaches children to take risks and not to fear getting wrong answers.

In brief, healthy motivation—perseverance, effort, and willingness to take risks—is associated with successful learning of mathematics.

Cognitive Flexibility

Children also learn that there are often many ways to approach and solve problems. This way of thinking promotes cognitive development and respect for diversity of thought.

Physical and Perceptual Skills

Throughout Big Math for Little Kids, children develop gross and fine motor skills as they learn how to manipulate large and small objects. In level K, Unit 1, *What Are Numbers?*, children learn how to write numbers. They also use different body movements to illustrate decades as they learn to count. In Unit 2, *The Shape of Things*, and Unit 3, *Patterns Plus*, children develop their perceptual skills. They learn to perceive the features of shapes and the regularities that define patterns. Throughout Big Math for Little Kids, children are on the move, learning to perceive the world carefully.

The Teacher's Role

It is important that teachers attempt to create classroom learning environments in which these social, motivational, and cognitive behaviors can be developed. Teachers should aim at establishing a supportive environment that signals to children that they can all work together, discuss, try hard, take risks, and respect different approaches to learning and solving problems. In particular, teachers should communicate the expectation that all children can and will learn challenging mathematics.

The Role of Integrated Learning

In addition to a strong literacy component, Big Math for Little Kids makes ample use of the intrinsic connections between mathematics, art, music, and science. For example, art and its foundational skills of construction and perception are explored in *The Shape of Things*. Connections to art and music are found in *Patterns Plus*. *Measure Up!* provides an introduction to scientific explorations.

Building Language, Literacy, and Communication Skills

One of the core principles of Big Math for Little Kids is that active participation in mathematical activities can help develop children's language, literacy, and communication skills. Learning mathematics requires accurate use of language, for example, when labeling features of shapes and describing which object is heavier than another. It requires two types of literacy, understanding mathematical ideas expressed in the context of stories as well as reading and writing various symbols, such as the numeral 3 and the + sign. Learning mathematics also requires learning to communicate mathematical ideas to others. As a result, strong language, literacy, and communication components are built into the program.

Language

During the pre-kindergarten and kindergarten years, children clearly need to learn basic vocabulary to describe objects, people, and events in their world. Acquiring appropriate vocabulary is essential to learning mathematics as well and flows naturally from mathematical activities. Both the pre-kindergarten and kindergarten levels of Big Math for Little Kids develop and reinforce the learning of basic mathematical vocabulary. This vocabulary includes not only number words, but also terms about shape *(square, triangle);* operations *(in all, altogether, adding, subtracting);* pattern *(repeat, next);* space *(next to, to the left);* comparison *(same, different);* cause and effect *(because, since);* prediction *(could happen, will happen next);* duration *(takes longer, takes less time);* and verification *(check your answer, is correct, mistake).*

Big Math for Little Kids does not shy away from teaching the use of correct mathematical terms. If young children can say Tyrannosaurus Rex, they are also capable of calling a rectangular prism by its proper name. Children gain confidence by using "big" words. At both the pre-kindergarten and kindergarten levels, teachers and children are expected to use the appropriate mathematical terms. The use of these terms encourages precision in description and thought.

Literacy

Actively listening to and making sense of literature is a critical early literacy experience. Storybooks written specially for Big Math for Little Kids are read by the teacher to introduce and develop key mathematical concepts and skills. In accordance with research on early literacy, teachers should use the storybooks to foster children's thinking and learning. For example,

- teachers should pause at key points in the story to let the children discuss the characters and their actions, and make predictions about what will happen next;
- teachers should help children to explore and make sense of the meaning of new words and concepts, and relate them to prior knowledge and experience;
- teachers should provide the children with opportunities to retell the story and use the story's new words.

To foster literacy, Big Math for Little Kids also identifies widely available storybooks, songs, and rhymes that can be used to further develop and reinforce key mathematical concepts and ideas.

The early learning of mathematics requires the reading and writing of basic symbols. Pre-kindergarten children easily learn to read the numerals 1 to 20 and often beyond. Kindergarten children often learn to read numerals to 100. Big Math for Little Kids also helps children to read and understand other symbols such as = and + and to write the basic numerals and signs.

To summarize, Big Math for Little Kids has been designed to enhance children's literacy skills. Accordingly, it is not necessary to make a choice between teaching young children mathematics or literacy. Experience with one can help children with the other.

Communication

Providing young children with ample opportunity to discuss their experiences, make predictions, justify their solutions, and engage in dialogue in small groups is central to the Big Math for Little Kids early literacy experience. This is accomplished in a number of ways. For example, in *What Are Numbers?*, level Pre-K, children arrange sets of picture cards to tell a story and then identify the events that occur first, second, third, and last. In *Measure Up!*, level K, children are asked to construct meaningful explanations of an improbable picture of a frog on the low end of a seesaw and a bear on

the high end.

Throughout the program, children work in small groups with the teacher and engage in continual exchanges of math talk. The teacher often finds it helpful to ask questions that

- ask for more information or explanation. For example, "Tell me about what you did." "Tell me more." "Why did you do that?"
- ask for speculation or prompt hypothesis information. For example, "What do you think will happen next?" "What do you think the next color will be?" "What do you think will happen when I do this?"
- ask for detection of errors and of ways to correct them. For example, "What is wrong with my counting?" "Can you fix it?"
- ask to follow and explain another child's line of reasoning. For example, "What do you think Sam was thinking when he said . . .?" "Why do you think Sam did that?"

Questions and statements of this kind are included for teachers within activities. They are shown in boldface text so they can be referred to more easily.

Asking these types of questions helps children learn how to describe and explain what they are doing and thinking, make and verify predictions, and discuss and consider alternative explanations. In accordance with the NCTM Communication standards, "math talk" fosters important language skills and helps children develop important metacognitive skills such as describing and justifying their thinking.

Meeting Children's Needs

Meeting Diverse and Common Needs Within Your Classroom

Big Math for Little Kids has been designed to enable all children, regardless of achievement level and native language, to be successful learners of mathematics. The activities provide for different levels of challenge. Most activities have two or more tasks. Each task presents a part of the development of a key concept or skill, and in general, each task is more complex than the task immediately preceding it. This organization provides for flexibility of instruction; children can be working on the same topic, but at different levels of difficulty, at the same time. Within the activities, there are often questions that guide children to understand the important ideas. Three types of assessment strategies help you gain insight into children's achievement and suggest ways to help individual children learn.

To engage children, activities are designed to capitalize on children's interests and to connect with daily classroom activities. For example, during the development of Big Math for Little Kids, the authors observed children using both patterns and symmetry in their block constructions. In developing the unit on patterns, the authors utilized children's natural interest in patterns but incorporated a variety of patterns—color, shape, number, letter, and sound—that are more complex than those children normally use or encounter.

Several activities take advantage of children's interests in dramatic play, drawing, and singing. Children mimic a balance beam in the activity Heavy as an Elephant. They dramatize stories like *Acorn Hunt* to explore addition and subtraction. They dance to "The Math Step" and "The Hokey Pokey" to develop understanding of the terms *forward, backward, to the left,* and *to the right.*

Providing sufficient time for all children to explore and wrestle with important mathematical ideas is critical. All children desire and need repetition of activities. All children need time to learn new vocabulary. All children need time to apply what they have learned. The planning chart at the beginning of each unit shows when activities should be introduced and identifies core activities that, once introduced, should be repeated regularly for the remainder of the year.

Multisensory Learning

For many children, multisensory explorations enhance learning and recall. Associating different body movements and voices with the decades helps children remember the counting sequence. Using different body movements to dramatize large numbers helps children differentiate hundreds from tens and tens from ones. Feeling shapes helps children differentiate triangles from squares and squares from nonsquare rectangles. Shaking and waving hands helps children distinguish their right from their left hand.

The Spectrum of Achievement Levels

Two features of the activities, Field-Test Notes and More to Do, target children currently at different places in the achievement spectrum. Some Field-Test Notes offer suggestions of ways to help children who may experience difficulty with some aspect of a particular activity. More to Do offers ways to extend or broaden the explorations of children who are able and eager for greater challenges.

Meeting the Needs of English-Language Learners

Many children begin school with a language other than English, so their learning task is even more complex than that of children who are native English-speakers. English-language learners (ELL students), who of course vary in English proficiency, must learn the academic content and a new language at the same time.

Big Math for Little Kids is designed to maximize English learning in mathematics by employing several teaching strategies that are effective with young English-language learners as well as native speakers.

Manipulative Materials and Visual Aids

Building the basic and conceptual vocabulary for mathematics is crucial for developing more than rote understanding. Visual aids such as pictures, photos, and posters as well as manipulatives such as counters, connecting cubes, and attribute blocks are essential for ELL students' comprehension. These aids can assist children in moving successfully from the concrete to language and symbols that are essential to mathematics.

Activities and Group Interaction

Having children work in small groups to solve problems and to show what they know sets up a natural environment for practicing English. For example, when small groups of children hunt for objects that are about 1 inch long, they spontaneously use measurement terms in a meaningful context. When children are expected to talk in a group about a math problem, share their results, and demonstrate their understanding by using manipulatives and symbols, all children, including English-language learners, benefit.

Active Physical Participation in Learning

When children are physically engaged in a mathematics activity, the teacher is sometimes able to see if a child comprehends the concept. For example, when a child is engaged in playing the pre-kindergarten pattern activity Math Hopscotch, the teacher can draw conclusions about the child's understanding of number patterns by observing the child as he or she jumps to show a pattern. Activities that involve physical participation often require little verbalization from the young ELL student.

Mathematical Vocabulary and Assessment

The Language of Mathematics section in each activity lists mathematical vocabulary and symbols that are important for all students to learn. Big Math for Little Kids assists ELL students in learning mathematical vocabulary by providing a variety of ways to learn the terms and frequent opportunities to practice them.

In addition, the program offers teachers many and varied opportunities to assess children's learning and thus to stay well informed of the progress ELL students are making in acquiring mathematical concepts and vocabulary.

Chants, Songs, and Rhymes

The songs and poems within the program provide opportunities for acquiring and practicing math concepts and language. Songs such as "If You're Happy and You Know It" also lend themselves to gestures and dramatization which support understanding of number and spatial terms.